Contents

Preface

The term *Islamism* refers to an effort, or movement, to align a state's internal structures with traditional Islamic precepts. Applicable state structures may include all elements of the government but especially the judicial branch, as well as educational, financial, and social institutions. Islamism is different from Islamic *fundamentalism* in that the latter refers more to an effort, to align society, not state structures, with Islamic precepts. Fundamentalism attempts to mold the norms and values of society rather than changing a state's formal institutions. Islamism and fundamentalism can be viewed as opposite ends of a continuum. The multitude of Islamic movements fall somewhere on this continuum, but will generally favor one pole or the other, although rarely to the complete exclusion of elements from the other. This paper addresses the Turkish political party Refah—an example of an Islamist movement. The Refah Party seeks to change Turkey's state structures from a secular to an Islamic orientation. The unique aspect of the Refah Party, in contrast to other Islamist organizations, is that it is operating within the constraints of the same secular, democratic political system that it seeks to change.

I gratefully acknowledge the guidance and assistance of Dr. Lewis Ware. His expertise inspired an interest in the topic and was invaluable in explaining its complexities.

Chapter 1

Origins

Introduction

The Refah Party is the only Islamist political party in Turkey. In recent years its popular support has increased, leading to a majority position relative to other parties in the Turkish parliament in 1995. The subsequent privilege of establishing and leading a coalition government is an unprecedented amount of responsibility earned by an Islamist party in Turkey. Since modern Turkey was founded on strict secular principles designed to keep religious influences out of government, the success of Refah raises questions regarding its nature: what does it stand for, who leads it, who belongs to it, where is it going? This paper addresses these questions and is organized into four chapters. Chapter 1 presents some background information about the Turkish secular state, the founding of Refah, the rise of Islamic influence, and the recent success of the Refah Party. That Islamist movements are gaining momentum in nations with repressive or autocratic regimes is no surprise; in contrast, the success of an Islamist party in a secular state founded on the principles of Kemalism does seem surprising until the underlying issues are examined. Chapter 2 discusses the ideology of Refah, specifically as it applies to issues regarding the democratic, secular state, society, economics, and foreign affairs. The Refah political platform is in most aspects completely opposite traditional modern Turkish policies; it seeks to minimize Western influence, provide a state structure sympathetic to the spiritual needs of its Muslim population, and foster relations and trade with other Islamic countries. How Refah hopes to achieve these goals is addressed in Chapter 3, which presents information about party leadership and organization. Much of Refah's success can be attributed not to the popularity of its political platform, but to its effective administration in public office—a trait woefully lacking in the mainstream parties. Refah's grassroots campaign efforts also make the party readily identifiable—and accountable—to the electorate. Finally, Chapter 4 comments on the future viability of the Refah Party. Whether it can build a sincere support base for its policies, as opposed to a protest support base, depends in large part on how well it can blend the many opposing viewpoints on controversial issues. Ultimately, the reader should be able to conclude that the Refah Party, although not unique from other Islamist movements in its ideological goals, is a unique product of Turkish politics and internal state issues. The constraints of a secular, democratic state, a fragmented political party structure, a precarious economy, and a watchful military all serve to temper Refah's conservative ideology into more pragmatic actions. The Turkish context surrounding the development of the Refah Party is important in understanding its nature and in predicting future success.

Origins

This chapter will briefly review the historical development of the Turkish secular state, discuss the origins of the Refah Party, describe the rise of Islamic political influence, and suggest some underlying causes for recent Islamist success.

Modern Turkey was formed out of the defeated Ottoman Empire. In that empire, the Sultan ruled from Istanbul; geographically, Turkey was the "home province" of a very large political territory. Unlike many neighboring "provinces," Turkey's population included influential political, economic, military, and religious elites who were familiar with the tasks and responsibilities of governing a large territory, and the commensurate glory and prestige. It is therefore not surprising that plans for a new Turkish government were underway well before the empire finally crumbled and that a charismatic Turkish leader would emerge from the influential elite with the intention of reestablishing a strong Turkish state. The successful ascension of a Turkish government effectively precluded the colonization of Turkey by European nations after World War I, in contrast to many of the neighboring states.

Mustafa Kemal, a distinguished military general responsible for securing Turkish independence upon the breakup of the Ottoman Empire, essentially established the new Turkish Republic. He was able to effectively transfer his reputation as a fierce, loyal commander into political legitimacy in the vacuum left by the Sultan. A nationalist at heart, he was driven by a tremendous ambition to establish a strong, united, modern Turkish state, and not let the greatness of the deposed empire slip away from the Turks. He was fortunate in having the intellect, charisma, determination, and support which enabled him to consolidate political power and pursue his goals. In doing so, he took for himself the name he is best known as: *Atatürk*—father of the Turks. His vision for Turkey's future focused on "replacing the country's Islamic traditions with principles of republicanism, nationalism, populism, and state control."[1] For Atatürk, a secular state was compelling and served two functions: "to forge a nation-state out of the multi-ethnic

3

remnants of the Ottoman Empire, and to combat all claims of disparate ethnic identities."[2] It is in this context that the exchange of Islamic conventions (e.g. government, law, language, alphabet, calendar, dress) for secular ones should be understood. "The aim of those changes was to diminish the influence of Muslim culture and weaken the power of tradition."[3] Under Atatürk, Islam officially became a private religion rather than a community religion, and was ostensibly replaced by "six fundamental and unchanging principles of the regime: Republicanism, Nationalism, Populism, Statism, Secularism, and Revolutionism/Reform."[4] In the process, Turkey became arguably one of the most modern, progressive Islamic states.

Although established as a democracy in 1922, Turkish government under Atatürk was essentially an autocracy with only one authorized party and Atatürk as President. When Atatürk died in 1938, he was succeeded by his Prime Minister Ismet Inönü, who served as President until 1950. In 1946, Inönü abolished the one party system, and numerous political parties were rapidly formed.

Despite Atatürk's efforts, the secularization of Turkey was incomplete. "Although the new, secular way of thinking gained acceptance in the middle class as well as among civil servants, government officials, and military officers, it barely penetrated the villages of the Anatolian hinterland."[5] In the population there, the values and traditions of Islam remained as strong as ever, and those interests eventually found expression in political parties. One of the first was the Democratic Party (DP), which won the 1950 elections. The DP administration "identified itself with the countryside, with agrarian interests, and with the rural population. Its approach to religion involved the incorporation of Islam as a living cultural tradition into the mainstream of Turkish politics, .and emphasized that religious commitment and social development were not incompatible objectives….Religion was increasingly invoked by the DP as a means of social and political control"[6] and eventually raised concerns among senior army officers that the secular principles of the state were in danger. In 1960, therefore, the army staged a successful coup, "claiming that the regime had betrayed Atatürk's principle of secularism."[7] After a short period of military rule, new elections were held and democratic government resumed. That the army did not impose a permanent administration reflects the degree of assimilation within the army of Atatürk's principles. The reverence for Atatürk within the army—partly because of his roots in the military— established the army's on-going role of protector of the secular state.

Military intervention in government represents a recurring theme in recent Turkish history. The military, particularly senior officers, together with influential, appointed state officials independent from party politics, such as judges or other leaders of important institutions, have repeatedly exercised a censorship of politics when the secular nature of the state seemed threatened. These individuals acting collectively as state elites and supported by the army have served to counteract the Islamist efforts of popularly elected officials in the political arena. In doing so, the state elites have effectively used their relatively independent, permanent institutions to circumvent the democratic process and preserve the status quo as established by Atatürk. "The state elites took it upon themselves to protect the early Republican ideals; hence, the three military interventions (1960-61, 1971-73, 1980-83) were undertaken in order to reinstitute those early ideals that the political elites had ostensibly ignored."[8] The interventions disrupted the development of the political parties and explain, at least in part, the fragmented political spectrum in Turkey today. "Among the consequences of this imposed reengineering of the Turkish political process was the splintering of both the main center-right and the center-left parties, and the development of constant internecine fighting among these parties for supremacy."[9]

The Refah Party (RP) is one such party. Its beginnings can be traced to 1970, when Necmettin Erbakan founded the National Order Party.[10] The National Order Party became the National Salvation Party (NSP) in 1972, and was represented in Parliament between 1973 and 1980, taking part in three different coalition governments.[11] The NSP was a conservative, right wing party that favored a revived Islamic consciousness: "Erbakan has consistently underscored the importance of Islamic values and repudiated the strict secularism of the Kemalist state that prevents ordinary Turks from expressing their cultural heritage."[12]

During the 1970s none of the various political parties were able to consolidate power, the result being a series of weak coalition governments. By 1980 the political situation in Turkey had become very unstable and polarized; political violence became so bad that the military once again intervened, claiming among other reasons the "threat of radical Islam as embodied in Erbakan's National Salvation Party."[13] The military government disbanded all political parties, including the NSP, and banned all former politicians from future political activities. Erbakan spent most of the time between 80 and 83 in military barracks.[14] The government also made significant changes to the constitution in an effort to introduce greater stability; for example, "changes to the 1982 constitution curbed the number of categories of the state elites, that is, appointed rather than elected bureaucratic and military elites,"[15] and mandated religious education in primary and secondary

6

schools.[16] The constitutional changes attempted to consolidate power available to political entities and simultaneously assert control over the influence of Islam. By legitimizing certain aspects, like education, guidelines and rules could be established; similarly, the emphasis of traditional Islamic values could serve to dampen dissent against the state. The constitutional changes were therefore designed to stabilize the political environment and minimize the necessity for future interventions. Ironically, the net effect of the military government's changes increased the overall influence of Islam—exactly what the NSP had been striving for. "It was under the rule of the National Security Council between 1980-83 that the Islamists achieved their greatest influence within the state apparatuses specializing in administration and ideology. The military junta launched an effort to modify the official ideology of Kemalism—which they felt was unnecessarily revolutionary in some of its aspects—with a 'Turkish-Islamist synthesis'."[17]

In 1983 the ban on political parties was lifted, although the old parties and politicians were still prohibited. Out of 15 parties formed, only three were allowed to contest in the 1983 elections. At this time, Erbakan established the Refah (Welfare) Party, essentially the same party as the NSP but with a different name. It was prohibited from participating in the 1983 elections but did participate in subsequent ones, gradually building an increasing support base.

The winner of the 1983 elections was the center-right Motherland Party (MP), led by Prime Minister Turgut Özal, who had been a member of the NSP in the 1970s. Under Özal's leadership, Islamic influence gained even more strength. Özal said "that secularism could not be considered as a restrictive element 'which will prevent protection of moral values, bar the way to religious activities and religious culture' and he stressed the

7

importance of religious instruction in schools in order 'to raise steady, virtuous generations'."[18]   Under Özal, "*tarikats* (religious orders) were encouraged as a counterweight to leftists,"[19] and many government posts within his administration were filled with associates sympathetic to his cause.[20] Özal especially nurtured his relationship with the Nakshbendi Sufi order, because "initiation of an export-led growth strategy necessitated an aggressive search for foreign customers who, in the 1980s, were found mainly in the Middle East. The Nakshbendis, with links to the Gulf states, were expected to play a significant role in promoting Turkish exports to the region and maintaining steady oil supplies."[21]   Özal also sanctioned the reestablishment of the *imam-hatip* (religious functionary) schools and granted them high-school equivalence, which allowed thousands of students to attend schools in-residence and helped to sponsor them in universities. This sponsorship is important because "many of the *imam-hatip* school graduates make their careers in civil service and certain ministries, such as Education and Culture. For example, in 1992, 60 percent of the Ankara University political science students were *imam-hatip* school graduates."[22]   Özal also allowed the introduction of Islamic banks to Turkey. Eventually, Özal's religious conservatism alienated him from part of his party, and the rift forced him to tone down some of his policies. Nevertheless, Özal contributed significantly toward legitimizing political Islam and his religious initiatives served to strengthen the roots of Islam within Turkey.

The political background just presented exposed the underlying historical conflict between secularism and Islamism and described a few examples of how organizations within the state have tried to resolve the conflict to their satisfaction. Key among these resolution efforts has been the easing of secular constraints in an accommodating effort to preclude extremism. The accommodation, however, has provided Islamists a strong base of support, and helps to explain the success of the Refah party, whose development and growth will be discussed now.

As stated earlier, Refah was established in 1983, and Erbakan regained legitimate leadership of the party in 1987, when a national referendum repealed the prohibition on former political leaders imposed in 1981. Throughout the remainder of the decade, Refah contested in elections and showed minor gains in vote percentages; in comparison to the major parties the percentages were insignificant. In the 1994 local elections, however, RP gained 19.1% of the vote,[23] and more importantly, won mayorships in Istanbul, Ankara, and 400 other cities and towns, including 28 of the 76 provincial capitals.[24] Since Turkey's population of 63 million is now over 75% urban (the six largest cities account for more than half of Turkey's population), with over 12 million living in Istanbul alone,[25] the winning of the mayoral contests allowed Refah to get a foot in the door and demonstrate its abilities to the Turkish population.

In December 1995, parliamentary elections were held a year earlier than scheduled because the two-year coalition government between the True Path Party (TPP, center-right) and the Republican People's Party (RPP, center-left) collapsed. In this election, Refah won the most votes and the largest representation in the Grand National Assembly, with 21.4% and 158 of 550 of the available seats. The Motherland Party and True Path Party were the second and third place finishers. Since MP and TPP both represent center-right positions, it made sense for these two parties to join forces, and in the two months following the election, negotiations eventually led to a coalition government between the MP and TPP. This coalition, however, only lasted until June; personality conflicts between party leaders and charges of corruption against Tansu Çiller, leader of TPP, escalated until the MP finally terminated the coalition by resigning in protest. Shortly thereafter, RP and TPP formed a coalition. "Under the coalition agreement, Erbakan will serve for two years as prime minister before rotating the jobs with TPP leader Çiller, who currently serves as foreign minister."[26]

The Refah Party's recent success can almost be considered predictable, given the political, religious, and social environment in Turkey. In the political environment, Refah capitalized on the fractionalized spectrum of parties and public disenchantment over the inability of previous regimes, particularly the Motherland and True Path Parties, to solve social, economic, and corruption problems. In that sense, Refah benefited from the Turkish 'protest vote' of voters normally supportive of center-right parties like MP and TPP. In religion, Refah offered the public a platform more in line with the already increased role and visibility of Islam in society. And socially, Refah alone could point to a proven agenda aimed at improving the living conditions and social services of the millions of Turks crowding into the cities. As a whole, "the RP can be perceived as fruit from the performance failure of the Turkish right, which had been in power most of the time during the multiparty period. With a broadening power base, which includes the protest vote of those having suffered under competitive market conditions since 1980, the RP is the most serious competitor of all the parties on the right."[27]

Notes

[1] *The Europa World Year Book 1996*, (London: Europa Publications Limited, 1996), 3172.
[2] Ertugrul Kürkçü, "The Crisis of the Turkish State," *Middle East Report*, April-June 1996, 3.

Notes

[3] Sencer Ayata, "Patronage, Party, and State: The Politicization of Islam in Turkey," *Middle East Journal*, Winter 1996, 41.

[4] Ayshe Kadioglu, "The Paradox of Turkish Nationalism and the Construction of Official Identity," *Middle East Studies*, April 1996, 187.

[5] Arnold Hottinger, "Secularization and Re-Islamization in Turkey," *Swiss Review of World Affairs*, October 1996, 8.

[6] Ayata, 43.

[7] *The Europa World Year Book 1996,* 3172.

[8] Kadioglu, 189.

[9] Henri Barkey, "Turkey, Islamic Politics, and the Kurdish Question," *World Policy Journal*, Spring 1996, 46.

[10] Jeremy Salt, "Nationalism and the Rise of Muslim Sentiment in Turkey," *Middle East Studies*, January 1995, 15.

[11] Ayata, 52.

[12] Barkey, 47.

[13] Kürkçü, 5

[14] Hugh Pope, "The Erbakan Whirlwind Sweeps through Turkey," *Middle East International*, July 19, 1996, 3.

[15] Kadioglu, 189.

[16] Salt, 16.

[17] Kürkçü 5.

[18] Salt, 17.

[19] Marvine Howe, "Tension Between Islamists and Secularists Grows in Turkey," *The Washington Report on Middle East Affairs*, May/June 1996, 109.

[20] Ayata, 44.

[21] Ibid.

[22] Salt, 19.

[23] Ergun Özbudun, "Turkey: How Far From Consolidation?," *Journal of Democracy*, July 1996, 128.

[24] Salt, 22.

[25] "Turkey: The Elusive Golden Apple," *The Economist*, 8 June 1996, insert, 1.

[26] James M. Dorsey, "Islamist Prime Minister Faces Domestic Challenges, International Opportunities," *The Washington Report on Middle East Affairs*, August/September 1996, 45.

[27] Ümit Cizre Sakallioglu, "Liberalism, Democracy, and the Turkish Centre-Right: The Identity Crisis of the True Path Party," *Middle East Studies*, April 1996, 154.

Chapter 2

Ideology

What makes the Refah Party different from the other Turkish political parties? How does it intend to incorporate its Islamic ideology into a secular state? What role does the West play in its vision? This chapter will address these and other questions about its ideology and is organized into the following areas: the democratic state, society, economics, and foreign affairs.

Refah's political ideology rests on the foundation that the role of government is to serve the electorate. It sees the societal and economic woes of the country as results of the failure of the other political parties to faithfully serve the electorate. Because the other political parties have abdicated that responsibility due to self-serving interests or incompetence, Refah discounts not only the legitimacy of the other parties, but the entire political system. During the 1995 election campaigns, for example, Erbakan vocally denounced the current democratic status of Turkey, calling it "a fraud."[1] In his view, the needs and the will of the people, whom the democracy is supposed to be representing, are not being met by the current system.

In Refah's eyes, one of the primary purposes of democracy is to ensure individuals their right of freedom of conscience: "the right to live according to one's beliefs."[2] Refah believes, for example, that Muslims should have the right to wear traditional religious clothes, be entitled to resolve legal issues in Islamic courts, and be able to conduct business in concert with Islamic precepts. The current secular state precludes Muslims from doing so, hence the assertion of a fraudulent democracy.

Refah's position towards legitimate government is unique among the Turkish political parties. Its views flow directly from the Islamic emphasis on the importance of the community—to be a good Muslim, you not only must be individually faithful; you must also contribute to a faithful community. For Refah, the importance of the community takes priority over the state. The primary function of a state, therefore, is to guarantee the autonomy of each community. Refah's leadership seems to take that philosophy to heart, and is making honest efforts to prove its legitimacy by providing for its constituents. For example, "In municipalities controlled by the Refah party, the ethos of community service is reinforced by the establishment of *halk meclisi* (people's councils) through which people can present problems and grievances to local leaders. Refah supporters cite these as instruments of direct democracy."[3]

Since the secular Turkish state is not responsive to its Muslim community, Refah seeks to replace the current secular state structure with a pluralistic one. Under such a pluralistic structure, communities would have the right to establish their own desired social institutions, which would then be guaranteed by the state. Under Refah ideals, Turkey would thus be organized according to the desires of its individual communities. Those communities desiring an Islamic structure would have that; those desiring a secular structure, or any other type of structure, would have that as well. Such a state structure has been the historical norm for many Islamic regimes and is similar to the *millet* system under the Ottoman Empire. Under the *millet* system, the Ottoman Empire "allowed religious and national minorities to access their own national or religious courts of justice."[4]   Refah's proposed structure presumably assumes that the *millet* system was historically successful and could be replicated in present circumstances.   That Refah looks towards the example of the Ottoman Empire also suggests frustration with the inability of present political systems to reconcile the ideals of legitimate government, democracy, and Islam.

The feasibility of such a pluralistic structure is debatable. Some critics fear it expands the possibilities for fragmentation; consider Quebec, Canada as an example.   Others, especially minorities, see a separate-but-equal, pluralistic system as inherently discriminatory. Since Turkey's population is primarily Sunni Muslim, the Shi'ites and non-Muslim minority communities fear a loss of the equality guaranteed them under the secular state: "Minorities who have enjoyed relative equality and freedom in modern nation-states now fear that Islamization will mean a reversion to the tolerated, 'protected' status of religious minorities under traditional Islamic law. Non-Muslims belonged to a separate class of citizens who constituted their own community. In exchange for their allegiance to the state and payment of a poll tax, they were free to practice their faith and be governed by their religious leaders and laws in private life in such areas as worship, education, and family law. However advanced such laws may have been relative to their times, today minorities regard such treatment as second-class citizenship."[5] Refah claims "that democracy and pluralism preclude the forcing of Islamic precepts on people"[6], but the minorities remain unconvinced. Critics question Refah's sincerity towards democratic government as a whole, and think Refah is only using democratic methods to achieve an ultimate goal of dismantling democratic and secular institutions and replace them with an authoritarian, religious-based regime. They claim Erbakan's apparent willingness to work within the established system "is the result of *takiyye*, an Islamic concept that allows temporary dissimulation to safeguard a long-term religious goal."[7]

In view of Refah's political philosophy, it is now easy to understand why Recip Erdogan, the RP mayor of Istanbul, claims that "Refah is not just an alternative to the other parties, but to the political regime in Turkey itself,"[8] and why Erbakan asserts "It should never be forgotten that democracy is a means, not an end. The real end is the creation of a felicitous order (*saadet nizami*)." [9]

Having examined Refah's political views toward the role of government in the state, let's now see what their views are regarding Turkish society. Modern Turkey, as we have seen, was built on Kemalism, "the Turkish project of 'Westernization;' it was originally an attempt to forestall direct or indirect colonization by the West by adopting Westernization."[10] Refah, like other Islamist movements, denounces this fundamental concept and wants to shrug off the influence of Western society. "The rise of Islam," says Abdurrahman Dilpak, leading Islamic thinker, "is like the river coming back to its own bed."[11] And although Atatürk is venerated by the Turks for successfully pulling Turkey into the 20th Century, Erbakan doubts he would endorse the pervasiveness of Western influence in Turkish society, and asserts "if Atatürk still alive he would now join Refah, the only party that carries the banner of independence from the West."[12] "Ironically, Atatürk, who set the trajectory of Turkish modernization towards a zealous Westernization, had never abandoned the rhetoric of a synthesis between the West and Islam. In fact, he adopted for himself and for the Turkish military the title of '*gazi*' (connoting a crusading spirit shared by the Muslims who waged wars against the infidel)."[13]

Refah seeks to expand the role of Islamic institutions and activities within society, such as Islamic banks and schools, business associations, religious foundations, and social services. The gradual Islamization of the government bureaucracy is an important step towards the Refah goal of establishing an Islamic state. For example, Refah would like to see the prohibition of *imam-hatip* graduates from entering the military abolished.[14] Another area is education; Refah seeks to place a greater emphasis of Islam in the educational process. The Islamist dominance in the education ministry is already reflected in policies, textbooks, and teacher selection.

The role of women in society remains ambiguous in Refah's social platform. Women's rights are not clearly articulated in party rhetoric, and Refah has no women in the party leadership. Similarly, it has refused to nominate women as candidates.[15] Perhaps this is because women are not interested in pursuing such roles in the party, although that seems unlikely, since at the grassroots level, women constitute a very important segment of the party work force. A more likely reason stems from traditional Islamic values, which relegate women to narrow public roles. The willingness of today's modern, well-educated Turkish women to conform to more traditional roles is questionable, especially given the successful examples of current leaders like Tansu Çiller, but in this area Refah will probably remain true to its conservative support base.

In keeping with the Islamic emphasis on community, Refah takes its role of serving the electorate seriously. At the local level, it has aggressively worked to provide improved social services, and it has succeeded. For example, "Refah has been tackling critical issues long ignored by the other parties, such as corruption, plight of the urban poor, growing lawlessness and social chaos in large cities."[16] In Istanbul, Refah Mayor Erdogan proudly asserts "'Before we came to office, there was widespread corruption and bribery; now many people are in jail and we have a clean administration.' He can point to other accomplishments: removal of 'hills of garbage,' provision of more seajets and seabuses to ease traffic congestion and work nearly completed on the light rail; refurbishing the city's water supply; tackling pollution problems by increased use of natural gas and stopping trucks from bringing in poor coal."[17] The success of Refah in this area is widely acknowledged: "Since the local elections in March 1994, Refah Party mayors have offered better services than their predecessors and worked hard to improve public services. They have reduced corruption and nepotism in the municipalities and acted more professionally than other parties on the left and right."[18] Refah is acknowledged with providing municipal services to working class neighborhoods. Such work, however, is not limited just to elected officials. One of Refah's strengths its army of party workers, whose work will be described in greater detail in Chapter 3. These party workers not only spread Refah's message but also provide a host of services, such as help finding jobs and health care, social services, and living necessities.

Refah extends its community-based ideology to the divisive Kurdish problem as well. They oppose the war against the Kurds, which costs the country $7 billion a year,[19] and also the Kurdistan Workers Party (PKK), instead offering "a platform of unity between Turkish, Kurdish, and other ethnic groups on the basis of Islam. Refah proposes official recognition of a distinct Kurdish ethnic identity and freedom of linguistic and cultural expression."[20] That degree of ethnic accomodation is surprising for an Islamist movement;

generally, Islamists are not normally sympathetic to minority concerns because it risks diluting the nature of the Islamic state. The subjugation of Islam to culture raises fundamental questions about the legitimate *umma*, of which there can only be one. How Refah reconciles this apparent contradiction is unknown. The Kurds themselves aren't sure what to make of Refah; some endorsed Refah with their votes during the last election, others see Refah's success as a threat to their protected status as a minority under a secular state.

To understand Refah's positions regarding economic policy, it is important to first understand some fundamentals about the Turkish economy. It suffers from "massive deficit spending, stubbornly high unemployment, a collapsed currency, and double and triple-digit inflation."[21] In 1994, the economy collapsed due to lack of confidence from international creditors, but it recovered quickly with very little outside help, and continues to move ahead, averaging an annual growth rate of 4-5 percent.[22] "Inflation hovers between 60-90 percent, the 1996 deficit was $15 billion (twice that of 1995), and a huge black economy and an inefficient tax-collection system compound the difficulties. Half of Turkey's manufacturing industry and 60 percent of its financial sector is still owned by the state."[23] At the same time, the economy is dependent on exports, 60 percent of which are with the European nations.[24] Refah's supporters tend to be the same as those who keep the economy going: "multitudes of small businessmen who represent a growing sector of the Turkish economy as a result of Özal's open-door trade policies of the late 1980s. These businessmen do not want state intervention in the economy and are therefore the main supporters of economic liberalization. For them, Islamic symbols and ethics are the best weapons to generate public opinion against statism and big industrialists."[25]

The problems saddling Turkey's economy are rooted in both history and politics. As reported by *The Economist* in "Turkey: The Elusive Golden Apple," in the Ottoman Empire, Turks were not businessmen, they were farmers and soldiers. Business was conducted by Greeks, Jews, and Armenians. Because of this, when the modern Turkish Republic was formed, many industries were nationalized, to assure their independence from outside investments. Additionally, the economy was bolstered with strong protectionist policies designed to foster the growth of fledgling Turkish businesses. During Özal's administration, efforts were made to reform the economy, and some protectionist policies were reversed. Those reforms, however, essentially ended after his administration, and the current situation is the result of the fragmented political arena. Because political parties are unable to gain a majority in parliament, coalition governments are required, and these tend to change relatively frequently. Consequently, economic policies tend to focus on the near-term, resulting in an erratic economy.[26]

To combat these difficulties, Refah proposes *Adil Duzen*, a Just Order. Specific areas that will be expanded upon here include proposals to promote individual enterprise, the replacement of a capitalistic economy with one based on Islamic concepts, and the limiting of state involvement to key activities like infrastructure and maintaining order.

Refah pledges support to the Turkish businessman, and wishes to promote private enterprise and individual initiative. It believes that small and medium sized businesses, if allowed to thrive, provide the best opportunity for Turks to progress and live prosperously. Erbakan has historically always supported the small businessman; he first asserted his leadership in the late 1960s when "he organized Anatolian businessmen against their much larger, domineering Istanbul counterparts."[27] During his campaign he

19

promised cheap loans for small businesses, and proposed cancellation of farming debt interest. Along similar lines, he opposed Turkey's recent membership into the European Customs Union, claiming that Turkish businesses would be undermined by cheaper European imports.

Membership into the Customs Union was successfully negotiated in December 1995 by True Path Party leader Tansu Çiller. Membership in the union is considered by Turkey's secular leaders "to be a prerequisite to full membership in the European Community and as the fulfillment of their quest to be part of the West."[28] "Under the terms of the union, effective 1 January 1996, Turkey will remove tariffs on European manufactured goods, which presently average 14%. Within a five-year grace period, Turkey will align its commercial laws with those of the EC."[29] Refah opposed the customs union in part because it creates the potential for increased imports from Europe. One of Refah's primary objectives is to decrease Turkey's dependence on trade with Europe, although the practicality of this objective is questionable since so much of Turkish trade is already with European countries.

Unlike those entrepreneurs yearning for even closer ties to the West, Refah sees the West as the cause of its economic second-rate status and cites capitalism as the principle reason for an unjust social and economic order. Membership in the EC, they think, is just another way for Western nations to continue their dominance of Islamic countries. "Erbakan charges that 'usurer capitalism' is an exploitive system run by imperialists and Zionists, and that their organization, the International Monetary Fund (IMF), pursues neo-colonialist policies through its austerity measures."[30] He also "holds on to a worldview in which Jews and Masons conspire to control the resources of the planet, and in which capitalism and communism are the mirror images of the same plot devised by Jews to advance their aims."[31]   Refah sees Israel as a pawn of the West, created and used to infiltrate the Islamic world and further capitalistic ventures and domineering schemes. Despite this adversarial approach to relations, Turkey does maintain Israeli business contracts and trade. As an alternative to the significant trade relations with Europe and the West, Refah proposes the establishment of an "Islamic Common Market,"[32] and "criticizes the government for failing to consolidate relations with the Black Sea Economic Forum and Islamic countries."[33] Refah believes that trade arrangements similar to the EU, but oriented east- and southward, would reassert Turkey's hegemony in the region, rather than perpetuate a second-rate role on the fringes of European economic policies.

Refah is supported in many of its views by businessmen with strong Islamic values. The primary example is MUSIAD, a Muslim business association founded in 1990 to promote a common commitment to Islamic values. As described by John Doxey in his article *Islamist Business Forges Ahead*, MUSIAD is aimed primarily at small to medium sized businesses. Its members strive to earn money the *helal* (righteous, religiously legitimate) way, by providing good pay and safe working conditions. Consisting of 2100 members, it is now considered the most influential Islamic voice on economic and political issues. MUSIAD and Refah see eye to eye on many issues. Both say Turkey should build stronger economic and political ties with Muslim nations, and both question the long-term value of Turkey's participation in Western alliances. Both groups oppose privatization of companies in strategic sectors like telecommunications and transportation, and both argue that the interest-based financial system fuels speculation by banks and investors, at the expense of Turkey's industrial development.[34]

Islamic banks offer one alternative to an interest-based financial system and receive Refah's endorsement. These banks were introduced into Turkey during President Özal's administration during the 1980s. "Islamic banks do not regard themselves as being mere financial institutions but as serving the broader goals of the Islamic society: the Islamic bank 'does not view economic development as separate from social development for to do so would be to put greater concerns on returns to the individual than society as a whole. Thus the Islamic bank should be as much a social bank as an economic or financial bank'."[35] These banks and the businesses they support are becoming increasingly common in Turkey.

Finally, Refah asserts a policy of a governmental role limited to providing state infrastructure, maintaining order, and withdrawal from all other economic activities. This role, however, and the relatively clear-cut anti-Western, pro-Islamic prose, has been somewhat contradicted by Refah's actions upon establishing an administration. Despite critique of the IMF, for example, Refah "is pursuing with the IMF a resumption of support for economic reform and a stabilization program that would turn the country's ailing economy around."[36] Since establishing his administration, Erbakan has "raised the salaries of several million civil servants by 50 percent rather than the budgeted 30 percent, and has said he would also seek parliamentary approval for a 30 percent bonus for members of the security forces. To help fund these expenditures, Erbakan has suggested selling state-owned land."[37] Refah no doubt has had to default on some of its economic reform rhetoric (such as the IMF) because it has no other choice in trying to keep the economy afloat, and will likely have just as much difficulty sticking to sticking to a firm economic program as every other party. It remains to be seen if Refah can make lasting reforms, resist populist, short term expenditures, steer economic arrangements away from the West, and still maintain a support base.

The final area of Refah ideology that deserves discussion is foreign affairs. In general, Refah's views towards foreign affairs parallel the broad anti-west, pro-Islamic stance already seen in its economic and social policies. But, as previously seen in other areas, Refah also seems to be willing to moderate its rather extreme rhetoric with significantly less extreme action since coming to power. The reasons for this stem from the reality of Turkey's geographical position. For example, Erbakan campaigned on platforms stating his intent to pull Turkey out of NATO, and to withdraw support for the US-led Operation Provide Comfort. Both of these platforms have since been retracted—Erbakan cannot escape the fact that Turkey owes its formidable military strength to support from the US and NATO. Erbakan actually helped to persuade the Turkish parliament to extend the mandate for Operation Provide Comfort.[38] Sacrificing military support and the ensuing strength derived from its Western allies in exchange of a more independent stance in international affairs would place Turkey in a precarious situation given neighbors like Iran, Iraq, Syria, Greece, and the Caucasian states of the former Soviet Union. Additionally, Erbakan must certainly realize that the strength of the Turkish military serves as a powerful glue that deters minority factions like the Kurds from declaring their independence. And, Erbakan certainly recognizes the military as a boundary not to be stepped over lest another intervention occur. Given this factor, Erbakan is not likely to do anything that would endanger the strength of the military.

23

Despite Turkey's role in NATO and its reliance on Western military support, Refah is striving to present an independent Turkish stance in international relations. Such efforts are in part motivated by a desire to secure the region and gain the support of hostile neighbors. For example, Erbakan has initiated efforts to establish a security cooperation agreement between Turkey, Syria, Iran, and Iraq. These efforts are not likely to be immediately fruitful, however, because of the strained relations over water rights and Turkey's role during Desert Storm. Syria, in particular, has protested the series of dams Turkey has built and is planning on building on the Euphrates River, fearing unacceptable water quantities and pollution.[39] Iraq has "foiled Erbakan's attempts to achieve security cooperation by intervening in internecine Kurdish fighting in allied-protected northern Iraq."[40]

Other relations attempt to assert Turkish independence and encourage economic relations. Shortly after Erbakan assumed his Prime Minister duties, he conducted controversial visits to Iran, Iraq, and Libya over the objections and protests of the US. These visits were "in part designed to placate his followers"[41] but also motivated by economics; for example, Turkey recently "signed a $20 billion, 22 year gas purchase agreement with Iran. Also signed were agreements to purchase electricity and boost bilateral trade. Erbakan said in reference to his newly arranged agreements with Iran that 'We cannot turn out backs on a crucial neighbor like Iran, especially when we need their energy resources. Turkey will not permit any third country to interfere in the growing trend of cooperation between Turkey and Iran'."[42] Turkey would also like to reestablish relations with Iraq; the international trade embargo has cost Turkey 20 billion dollars over the last five years.[43] Finally, despite the anti-Zionist rhetoric, Refah continues to cultivate economic and military relations with Israel and has negotiated business contracts for

Israeli maintenance support of Turkish avionics equipment.

Notes

[1] Ergun Özbudun, "Turkey: How Far From Consolidation?," *Journal of Democracy*, July 1996, 133.

[2] Ibid., 134.

[3] Sami Zubaida, "Turkish Islam and National Identity," *Middle East Report*, June 1996, 12.

[4] Richard Robinson, *The First Turkish Republic*, (Cambridge: Harvard University Press, 1965), 11.

[5] John L. Esposito, *Islam, the Straight Path*, (New York: Oxford University Press, 1991), 209.

[6] Zubaida, 11

[7] Hugh Pope, "The Erbakan Whirlwind Sweeps through Turkey," *Middle East International*, 19 July 1996, 3.

[8] Sabri Sayari, "Turkey's Islamist Challenge," *Middle East Quarterly*, September 1996, 39.

[9] Haldun Gülalp, "Islamist Party Poised for National Power in Turkey," *Middle East Report*, May-June/July-August 1995, 56.

[10] Ibid., 54.

[11] Marvine Howe, "Tension Between Islamists and Secularists Grows in Turkey," *The Washington Report on Middle East Affairs*, May/June 1996, 110.

[12] Gülalp, 56.

[13] Ayshe Kadioglu, "The Paradox of Turkish Nationalism and the Construction of Official Identity," *Middle East Studies*, April 1996, 191.

[14] Sayari, 37.

[15] Ibid., 40.

[16] Ibid., 37.

[17] Howe, 109.

[18] M. Hakan Yavus, "Turkey's 'Imagined Enemies': Kurds and Islamists," *The World Today*, April 1996, 100.

[19] "Turkey: The Elusive Golden Apple," *The Economist*, 8 June 1996, insert, 11.

[20] Gülalp, 55.

[21] Josh Martin, "Can New Government Re-open the Door to Prosperity?," *The Middle East*, April 1996, 19.

[22] "Turkey: The Elusive Golden Apple," 11.

[23] Ibid., 8-9

[24] Henri Barkey, "Turkey, Islamic Politics, and the Kurdish Question," *World Policy Journal*, Spring 1996, 49.

[25] Yavus, 100.

[26] "Turkey: The Elusive Golden Apple," 11

[27] Barkey, 48.

Notes

[28] Ibid., 43

[29] Martin, 20.

[30] Gülalp, 56.

[31] Barkey, 48.

[32] Gülalp, 56.

[33] Howe, 110.

[34] John Doxey, "Islamist Business Forges Ahead," *The Middle East*, June 1996, 18.

[35] Jeremy Salt, "Nationalism and the Rise of Muslim Sentiment in Turkey," *Middle East Studies*, January 1995, 20.

[36] James M. Dorsey, "With Friends Like Qaddafi, Islamist Erbakan Doesn't Need Enemies," *The Washington Report on Middle East Affairs*, November/December 1996, 37.

[37] James M. Dorsey, "Islamist Prime Minister Faces Domestic Challenges, International Opportunities," *The Washington Report on Middle East Affairs*, August/September 1996, 45.

[38] Dorsey, "With Friends Like Qaddafi," 37

[39] Hugh Pope, "Unedifying Race for Power," *Middle East International*, January 19, 1996, 13

[40] Dorsey, "With Friends Like Qaddafi," 37.

[41] Ibid.

[42] "Turkey's New Prime Minister Signs $22 Billion Energy Pact in Tehran," *Middle East Monitor*, August 1996, 62.

[43] Barkey, 50.

Chapter 3

Structure

In Turkey, political parties have historically been focused around a central leader. "One typical feature of all Turkish political parties has been the unquestionable authority of the leader unconstrained by party structures. The locus of power and initiative within the parties has always been in leadership characterized by personalistic decision-making and a monolithic internal structure."[1] Refah is no exception to this generalization; since its inception it has been Erbakan's party; he has set the course and steered the party through adversity.

Refah, however, is not monolithic; because it is currently the only party with an Islamist platform, it has attracted both members and supporters from a wide spectrum of ideology, "and carries within itself a variety of platforms."[2] Many supporters favor democratic ideals and the secular state; in fact, "a recent survey found that 41 percent of those who voted for Refah declared themselves as *laïk*."[3] (The term used in Turkish is based on the French *laïcité*, which denotes separation—the principle of separation between religion and state.[4]) Other supporters favor the institution of a fully Islamic state governed according to the *Shari'a* and a complete realignment of Turkish interests in the world. Between these two poles lie supporters of more moderate viewpoints. Because of such diversity, party members, either as elected officials or as campaigners, often send mixed signals to the Turkish population and the international community, making it difficult to determine exactly what, if any "official" position on a given issue is.

Necmettin Erbakan was born in 1926 "into a prosperous family and as a businessman accumulated considerable wealth. Trained as a diesel engineer, he worked and studied in Germany in the 1950s."[5] As already mentioned, he began a career of public service by organizing Anatolian businessmen into a union of sorts, and was first elected to Parliament in 1969. In 1970 he established the National Order Party, which was renamed the National Salvation Party in 1973. From 1973 to 1980, as the leader of the NSP, he participated in various coalition governments. After the military intervention in 1980, he was barred from politics but was still able to establish Refah. In 1987 he officially reemerged as Refah's leader. Currently 70 years old, "Erbakan is first and foremost a Turkish nationalist who wants to see Turkey as a leader of a political/economic Islamic bloc rather than remain a second rate power in the West."[6]

Erbakan represents the original, conservative element of Refah. "The leadership cadre around him is old and conservative. The younger generation of professional leaders, as represented by Erdogan, is more technocratic and 'modern' in its orientation….And then there is a hard-line core….Clearly, the party is ripe for a power struggle, which will probably erupt with Erbakan's death."[7] One possible successor to Erbakan is perhaps the second most important leader in Refah, Recip Tayyip Erdogan. A Marmara University graduate in economics and political science, Erdogan is the 41 year old mayor of Istanbul.[8] We have already addressed some of his successes in Chapter 2.

Perhaps Refah's greatest strength lies not in its leadership, but in its party workers. Among the all Turkish political parties, Refah has the largest number of party workers, and these party workers are the ones with whom the average Turkish citizen is most likely to have contact with. "The highly motivated, well-disciplined and strongly committed activists believe in their political cause as a mission ordained by God. They function at the community level, visiting every single quarter, street, and cluster of houses in the cities, gathering information about each voter and family separately, evaluating the data, and finding solutions for each problem. To penetrate small communities, the young activists, including an army of women who can arrange home visits at any time of the day, have emerged as the party's major assets. Reporters write that the party organization is on steam, as though an election is always imminent, carefully planning activities, minutely assigning responsibilities for each group and individual activist, and coordinating their efforts."[9]

The party workers rely on personal, face-to-face contact rather than mass media, and go door-to-door through the neighborhoods explaining the party's simple ideology. In poor neighborhoods composed of recent city immigrants, they also provide "health care and medical aid, help to children with their homework, assistance in finding jobs, food, fuel, and various commodities people need. Finally, and most important, they offer 'sympathy,' an appreciation of the difficulties of everyday life for ordinary people, respect for their work and their struggles."[10]

Despite these simple, old-fashioned campaign efforts, Refah also relies on modern technology and maintains computerized voter registration data bases. Sometimes the Refah records are more accurate than the official ones: several years ago these records were requested by the Istanbul administration when an explosion in one of the shantytowns resulted in a number of deaths—the records helped to determine who had

lived there at the time of the explosion.[11]

Refah would not be able to support such armies of party workers without adequate

financial support. So far, funding does not seem to be a problem, since "it is reportedly

the richest political party in Turkey today."[12] Accused of receiving funding from religious

groups from Iran, Refah denies such donations, which are illegal in Turkey, and claims

"most funds come from members (limited to $1200 a year), including Turkish workers in

Germany, and from religious and social foundations."[13]

Notes

[1] Ümit Cizre Sakallioglu, "Liberalism, Democracy, and the Turkish Centre-Right: The Identity Crisis of the True Path Party," *Middle East Studies*, April 1996, 145.

[2] Jeremy Salt, "Nationalism and the Rise of Muslim Sentiment in Turkey," *Middle Eastern Studies*, January 1995, 21.

[3] Sami Zubaida, "Turkish Islam and National Identity," *Middle East Report*, June 1996, 10.

[4] Bernard Lewis, "Why Turkey is the Only Democracy," *Middle East Quarterly*, March 1994, 46.

[5] Hugh Pope, "The Erbakan Whirlwind Sweeps Turkey," *Middle East International*, 19 July 1996, 3-4.

[6] Henri Barkey, "Turkey, Islamic Politics, and the Kurdish Question," *World Policy Journal*, Spring 1996, 48.

[7] Ibid.

[8] Marvine Howe, "Tension Between Islamists and Secularists Grows in Turkey," *The Washington Report on Middle East Affairs*, May/June 1996, 109.

[9] Sencer Ayata, "Patronage, Party, and State: The Politicization of Islam in Turkey," *Middle East Journal*, Winter 1996, 52.

[10] Ibid.

[11] Barkey, 45.

[12] Sabri Sayari, "Turkey's Islamist Challenge," *Middle East Quarterly*, September 1996, 36.

[13] Howe, 109.

Chapter 4

Outlook

Before any guesses regarding Refah's future can be advanced, it would be helpful to summarize concrete reasons for the party's recent success. These reasons have already been discussed in general, the following serves as a review. Six "specific catalysts responsible for the Islamic revival include 1) a crisis of legitimacy of political elites and social systems; 2) ineffective rulership; 3) excessive reliance on coercion for elite control; 4) class conflict in the midst of corruption; 5) military weakness and 6) the disruptive impact of modernization, with its non-Islamic ideologies, values, and institutions."[1]

Not all of these catalysts apply in Turkey, but certainly the leadership and legitimacy of the political parties, as well as the disruptive impact of modernization do. Refah has capitalized on public disenchantment with the other political parties; they have been unable to solve the social and economic problems arising from transformation of the nation from an agricultural to industrial base, and they have lost public confidence because of the corruption of the politicians. Refah has also capitalized on its unique ideology; it alone can point to a political agenda completely different from the rest of the field, and by doing so, it isolates itself from the other parties and their problems. Refah has also been able to organize and fund itself better than the other parties, and has found a successful formula for distributing its message by relating one-on-one to the electorate. Finally, Refah has been riding a rising wave of Islamic awareness and revival, not just in Turkey, but throughout the Islamic world. It has been able to capitalize on heightened religious values among the Turkish population and package those values in a marketable political platform. In order to remain viable, however, it must be able to balance opposing forces on a number of issues, or else risk dilution or extremism of its message.

First, Refah must balance divergent views within the party. The task of a political party to track a straight course is simple when it is not in power, since external forces can be ignored. Now that Refah has acquired a position of leadership, it finds itself having to compromise on issues, and this compromise may not be accepted by parts of the support base. For example, "Oriented as it is to electoral contest, Turkey's mainstream Islamist leadership is more open to political pressure and compromise than its counterparts elsewhere. This flexibility, however, is limited by the need to satisfy its core constituency. The question is whether pressures towards liberal moderation in the political sphere can hold back the social authoritarianism inherent in Islamist ideology and social ethics."[2] "So far, there seems to have been enough room inside Refah both for thorough-going Islamic radicals who admire Iran, businessmen who want to be in with the party of power, and a lot of people in between. The glue is Refah's popularity as a disciplined party less tainted than the others by corruption and good a mending potholes and keeping the streets clean."[3]

But besides just holding the party together, Refah must also balance its long-term goals for an Islamic state, first, against political opposition, by gaining and maintaining a greater support base, and second, against the threat of military intervention, which would likely eradicate the progress attained in the last 15 years. Economically, Refah must balance the reality of Turkey's extensive trade arrangements with the West against the desires for a more Islamic business structure and more trade with regional nations. Additionally, it must balance its willingness to improve social services and welfare with the ability of the state to fund such efforts. In relations with other nations, Refah must balance desires for greater international autonomy and closer relations with Islamic states against the need for Western military support and alliances.

For Erbakan, the tasks are clear: keep his party together and tread a moderate line to consolidate power and gain a greater share of parliamentary seats. Only then will he have the elbow room to fully pursue the ideological goals of the party. In the meantime, he should concentrate on balance: "The theme that a patriotic Turk should try to achieve a balance between the benefits of the West and East by opting for adopting the science and technology of the former and the spirituality of the latter is repeated quite often in the schooling system designed by the educational establishment in Turkey. This difficult endeavor is almost like a mission of every patriotic Turk."[4] So far, the Refah Party has shown a willingness to compromise, which explains the waffling on key issues—Refah is not so much an ideological, unbending elephant as a pragmatic and flexible snake.

Notes

[1] R. Hrair Dekmejian, "The Islamic Revival in the Middle East and North Africa," *Current History*, April 1980, 168.

[2] Sami Zubaida, "Turkish Islam and National Identity," *Middle East Report*, June 1996, 15.

[3] "Faces of Islam," *The Economist*, 17 August 1996, 44.

[4] Ayshe Kadioglu, "The Paradox of Turkish Nationalism and the Construction of Official Identity," *Middle East Studies*, April 1996, 177.

Chapter 5

Conclusions

The Refah Party is not unique from other Islamist movements in its ideological goals, but it is distinctly Turkish, seeking to create a strong, independent state. Its goals are primarily Islamist: it seeks to establish a legitimate government responsive to the needs of the society. It seeks to establish a thriving, independent state by securing its external borders and providing for internal stability. It seeks to diversify its economic and foreign relations beyond just the West; doing so would provide it with more options, greater opportunities, and potentially greater power and prestige. The fundamentalist goals of fostering an Islamic community and the values associated with it can be seen as complementary, but secondary, to the greater goals relating to the state.

Unlike some other Islamist movements, Refah is able to work within the state, and by doing so, "its re-Islamization of Turkey is fundamentally different from other nations: it does not have to declare the existing government heretical; rather, it needs only to call for a greater role of religion in society."[1] As part of the state political system, Refah is constrained by it; it must fight for votes like every other political party in Turkey, and try to survive in a volatile political atmosphere. Refah must also remain within the secular boundaries established by the constitution and enforced by the military.

For the Refah Party to enjoy future success, it must successfully balance its ideology against its existence, avoiding excessive compromise, which would dilute its efforts, and excessive extremism, which would result in its annihilation. Refah must also strive to maintain the unity and identity of the party, lest it succumb to the fate of other Turkish political parties, namely weakness, division, and ineffectiveness.

Notes

[1] Arnold Hottinger, "Secularization and Re-Islamization in Turkey," *Swiss Review of World Affairs*, October 1996, 9.

Bibliography

Ayata, Sencer. "Patronage, Party, and State: The Politicization of Islam in Turkey." *Middle East Journal*, Winter 1996, 40-56.

Barkey, Henri. "Turkey, Islamic Politics, and the Kurdish Question." *World Policy Journal*, Spring 1996, 43-52.

Dekmejian, R. Hrair. "The Islamic Revival in the Middle East and North Africa." *Current History*, April 1980, 168-174.

Dorsey, James M. "Islamist Prime Minister Faces Domestic Challenges, International Opportunities." *The Washington Report on Middle East Affairs*, August/September 1996, 45.

————. "With Friends Like Qaddafi, Islamist Erbakan Doesn't Need Enemies." *The Washington Report on Middle East Affairs*, November/December 1996, 37.

Doxey, John. "Islamist Business Forges Ahead." *The Middle East*, June 1996, 17-18.

Esposito, John L. *Islam, the Straight Path.* New York: Oxford University Press, 1991.

The Europa World Fact Book 1996. London: Europa Publications Limited, 1996.

"Faces of Islam." *The Economist*, 17 August 1996, 42-44.

Gülalp, Haldun. "Islamist Party Poised for National Power in Turkey." *Middle East Report*, May-June/July-August 1995, 54-56.

Hottinger, Arnold. "Secularization and Re-Islamization in Turkey." *Swiss Review of World Affairs*, October 1996, 7-11.

Howe, Marvine. "Tension Between Islamists and Secularists Grows in Turkey." *The Washington Report on Middle East Affairs*, May/June 1996, 24-110.

Lewis, Bernard. "Why Turkey is the Only Democracy." *Middle East Quarterly*, March 1994, 41-49.

Kadioglu, Ayshe. "The Paradox of Turkish Nationalism and the Construction of Official Identity." *Middle East Studies*, April 1996, 177-193.

Kürkçü, Ertugrul. "The Crisis of the Turkish State." *Middle East Report*, April-June 1996, 2-7.

Martin, Josh. "Can New Government Re-open the Door to Prosperity?" *The Middle East*, April 1996, 19-20.

Özbudun, Ergun. "Turkey: How Far From Consolidation?" *Journal of Democracy*, July 1996, 123-138.

Pope, Hugh. "The Erbakan Whirlwind Sweeps through Turkey." *Middle East International*, 19 July 1996, 3-4.

————. "Unedifying Race for Power." *Middle East International*, 19 January 1996, 12-13.

Robinson, Richard. *The First Turkish Republic.* Cambridge: Harvard University Press, 1965.

Sayari, Sabri. "Turkey's Islamist Challenge." *Middle East Quarterly*, September 1996, 35-43.

Salt, Jeremy. "Nationalism and the Rise of Muslim Sentiment in Turkey." *Middle Eastern Studies*, January 1995, 13-27.

Sakallioglu, Ümit Cizre. "Liberalism, Democracy, and the Turkish Centre-Right: The Identity Crisis of the True Path Party." *Middle East Studies*, April 1996, 142-161.

"Turkey's New Prime Minister Signs $22 Billion Energy Pact in Tehran." *Middle East Monitor*, August 1996, 62.

"Turkey: The Elusive Golden Apple."*The Economist*, 8 June 1996, insert 1-18.

"Welfare State." *The Economist*, 6 July 1996, 46-47.

Yavus, M. Hakan. "Turkey's 'Imagined Enemies': Kurds and Islamists." *The World Today*, April 1996, 99-101.

Zubaida, Sami. "Turkish Islam and National Identity." *Middle East Report*, June 1996, 10-15.

www.ingramcontent.com/pod-product-compliance
Lightning Source LLC
Chambersburg PA
CBHW081802280526
45789CB00008B/2968